Lovers Leap

Lovers Leap

Elizabeth Cusack

Copyright © 2024 by Elizabeth Cusack.

Library of Congress Control Number:	2023923913
ISBN: Softcover	979-8-3694-1304-3
eBook	979-8-3694-1303-6

All rights reserved. No part of this book may be reproduced or transmitted in any form or by any means, electronic or mechanical, including photocopying, recording, or by any information storage and retrieval system, without permission in writing from the copyright owner.

Any people depicted in stock imagery provided by Getty Images are models, and such images are being used for illustrative purposes only.
Certain stock imagery © Getty Images.

Print information available on the last page.

Rev. date: 12/12/2023

To order additional copies of this book, contact:
Xlibris
844-714-8691
www.Xlibris.com
Orders@Xlibris.com
857486

Biography

Elizabeth Cusack is a California native. Her California ancestors are Scots and Irish, pioneers in San Francisco during the Gold Rush years. Her father's side is Dutch and English; they settled in New York and fought the British in the Revolutionary War. In her first seventeen years, Elizabeth moved twelve times, living in various states across America and in three cities in the United Kingdom. She graduated high school in Seoul, South Korea. Elizabeth attended Northern Arizona University where she focused on literature and theater. At the age of eighteen, she began acting professionally. She attended the University of California at Santa Barbara and completed a Bachelor of Arts degree in Art. For decades Elizabeth performed on stage. *Lovers Leap* is her first book, inspired by the Greek poetess Sappho. Elizabeth has published numerous poems. Her next project is a one-woman play. She resides in California and New Mexico.

Acknowledgements

I wish to thank NJ Cusack for his care and support during the years 2020-2023 in which this book was written. I thank my classics professor, Barry B. Powell, for writing the foreword to *Lovers Leap* and offering his erudite advice. I am indebted to my employer, William M. Curtis, who taught me to edit, my poetry professor, Michael MacMahon, who declared I wrote publishable poems, and David L. O'Nan, Editor of *Fevers of the Mind*. Fragments of my poems published in *Fevers of* anthologies coalesce in *Lovers Leap*.

The fragments of Sappho's writing in this book were translated by Mary Barnard. The illustrations of Sappho and Phaon are by Amie Oliver. The painting is *Head of a Woman* by Jean Jacques Henner, Dayton Art Institute, courtesy of Wikimedia Commons.

Foreword

SAPPHO *REDUX*

by Barry B. Powell, Halls-Bascom Professor of Classics Emeritus at the University of Wisconsin-Madison, author of *Greek Poems to the Gods, Hymns from Homer to Proclus*

Elizabeth claims a sympathy with the ancient Greek poetess Sappho, and it's not hard to see why. She's asked me to say a few words about this most famous poet.

Sappho lived perhaps circa 630–570 BC, about five hundred years after the invention of the Greek alphabet, an invention that made her poetry possible. She lived on the island of Lesbos just off the Turkish coast, probably in the city of Mytilene. The ancients adored her and called her the Tenth Muse. She greatly influenced poets in later times, but oddly we know little about her poetry and little about her life. Most of her work was lost when scrolls were converted to codices beginning in the third century after Christ. Furthermore her poetry is in a difficult dialect, Aeolic, unfamiliar to readers accustomed to what had for long become the standard Attic Greek.

Though we know nothing real about Sappho's life, many traditions were attached to her. The earliest biography dates to the late second or third century AD, 800 or 1000 years after Sappho's career. She is said to be from a high-class family. She had three brothers, two now mentioned in a nearly complete poem (the "Brothers Poem") discovered in 2014. Because of local politics she was exiled to Sicily around 600 BC. A fragment of a play by Menander says that Sappho threw herself off of the cliff out of love for one Phaon, but this is unlikely to be true.

The words "sapphic" and "lesbian" are known to all, but the ancients never perceived her as celebrating homoerotic love. In comedy Sappho was portrayed as a promiscuous heterosexual "fox." The earliest references to discuss Sappho's homoeroticism come from the Hellenistic period (c. 321-31 BC), five hundred years after she lived. Her poems celebrate women's beauty and character, but these are evidently wedding songs that glorify the bride whom the groom will soon enjoy.

We call Sappho a lyric poet because her song was meant to be accompanied by a lyre, a sort of handheld harp with seven strings. Perhaps each syllable of the song was accompanied by the pluck of a string? Still, we are a bit mystified: Did a group of singers, a chorus, dance and sing, say, in praise of the bride, or did a solo singer stand in the middle of the ceremony and sing? And why does any written version survive? Probably the words were written down because more than one person had to sing them. Sappho's poetry are scripts for public performance no doubt by a chorus.

So when Sappho says "I" the whole group is speaking. By "I" she does not mean "I, Sappho" but "people like me who can feel like this." What is public epideictic poetry was early and consistently mistaken, up to recent times, for private expressions of personal emotion when really they are the expressions of universal sentiments.

But all we know about Sappho comes from a few fragments and one complete poem. Scholars estimate that she wrote 10,000 lines of poetry, of which only around 650 survive. Let us look at fragment 31 preserved but for the last stanza in the first-century AD in "On the Sublime," a treatise on aesthetics (my translation):

> That man seems to me to be like a god
> Who sits beside you and hears
> Your sweet talk
> And your delightful laugh

That broke
The heart in my chest.

For when I see you even for a moment
I cannot say a word.
My tongue is smashed,
A thin fire runs quickly under my skin,
I can see nothing!

There is a roaring in my ears,
Cold sweat runs down my back.
A trembling savages me,
I am paler than grass,
I am near death!
But all must be endured…

There it is — intense emotion of a frankly very modern form. Elizabeth's poems are very like this.

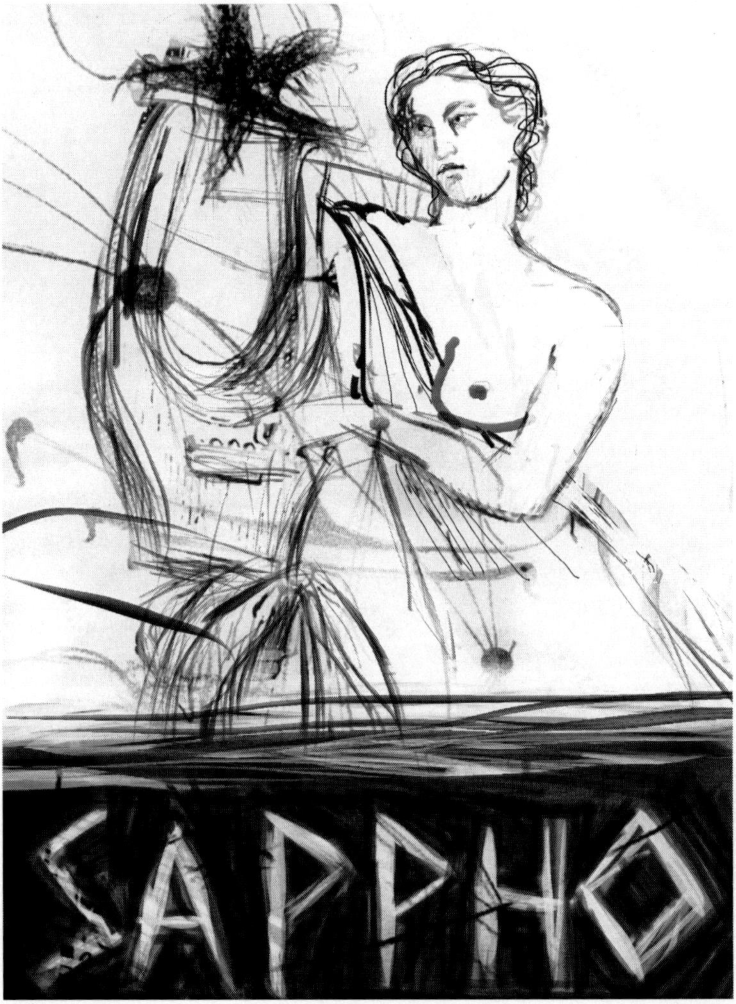
SAPPHO

*We shall enjoy it
As for him who finds
Fault, may silliness
And sorrow take him!*

Sappho

For Phaon

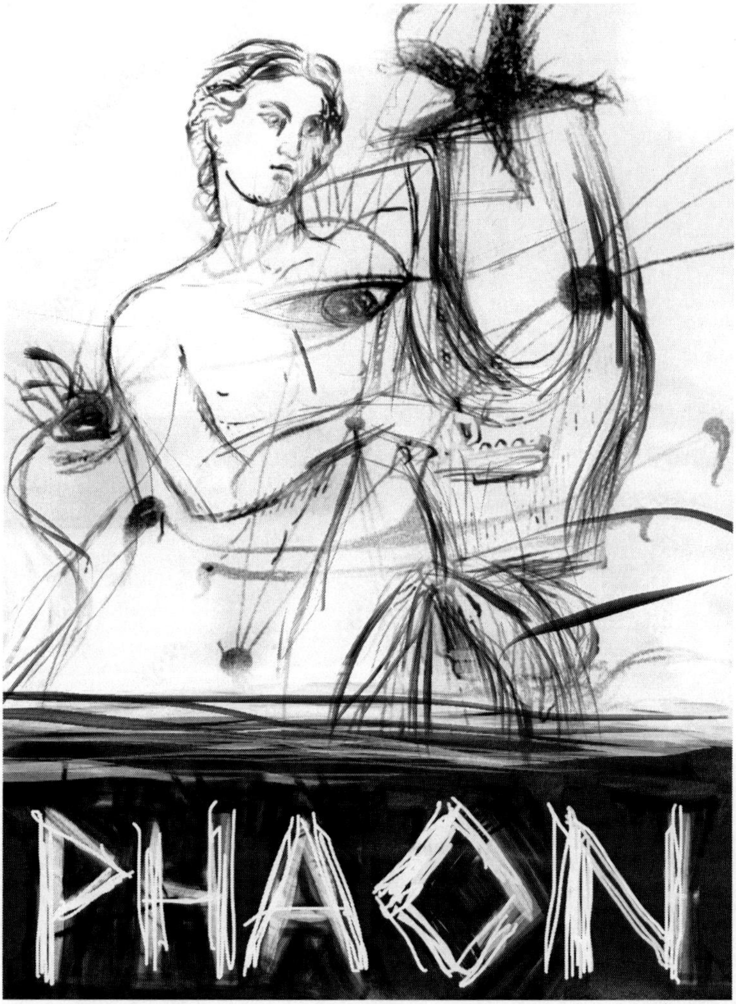
PHAON

Prologue

You are staring at me
With your intense eyes
You are just out of reach
We are nearly there
Your eyes are on fire
Who am I?
Who was I before?
When did I become
A part of your soul?
Our hearts beat side by side
Hello, beautiful creature!
I live with a thousand faces
On this island in the sea
Let's spin a song.

Before was a dream—
The sand, the wind, the future
My eyes are prisms now
I am floating in the universe
Where love began
You have the power
To throw me off
But you don't
I am welcome
In this lost land
I hold on tight
Am I going blind?
Am I seeing double?

You say I'll be alright
You say, whispering
What are you thinking?
Everything's fine
Please, no need to worry
We love that we love
We are together now
The sirens are singing
The cymbals are crashing
And the dancing never stops
I will not hurt my heart again
Inside of these stone walls
I will not disappear again
When I hear their applause
For the hearts I have broken
I'm sorry for them all.

See me at dawn under the trees
I am lunacy in ecstasy
Chains on my wrists
Bells on my feet
Music in my ears
I am sleepless and free
I come in a robe of fire
With beads of wood and silk
You touch me and say
I am here to stay
We will ride through the air
You see me and say my name
You feel me and know I am there
I touch your feet and say
You know my desire
Come and stay
It is not far away
Come for hours

Dream in this place
It is for you
My light at midnight
The lucid dreams
I will share with you
All my remaining days.

I

It's no use
Mother dear, I
Can't finish my
Weaving
You may
Blame Aphrodite
Soft as she is
She has almost killed me with
Love for that boy

Sappho

I flew to this island
Before I was born
I arrived in a whirring of wings
I was filled with love
I played on the beach
And life was as it should be
I play in the breeze
Watch the fruit fall
The hummingbirds sing in the trees
I touch thorns
I find feathers
Fallen nests and cracked eggs
Grandmother muses
Weaves garlands
Grandfather watches me dance

Dancing shoes are my first memory
Grandmother is seeing heaven
When she visits me
She tells me to run away
We walk out on to the rocks
She keeps me close
We visit her mother
She is blind and ancient
She touches me and says
I am the chosen one
When I learn they are gone
I weep and wail.

Father is on an endless campaign
Mother is nearly out of her head
She is always pretending
Jangling her bracelets and dancing around
She is rarely around
But I remember her gowns
I have a vision of her
When she was young
Lying in the sun
On a rock by the sea
She knew I was leaving
She sent me a letter later
Asking what had happened to me
I was too far away to reply.

The white birds cackle
I am floating in a boat
Alone with him
He has chosen me!
We sit quietly
The waves rock gently

He says, *See the dazzling display*
The thousands of lilies!
It is the prettiest thing I have ever seen
I am twelve years old
He possesses a quiet and watchful soul
Alabaster skin, long dark hair
He says, *See the beauty, hear the tranquility!*
Those mocking girls are not like you
In school, I weave a design
I stare at him and am seen
And when we go sailing, he chooses me
He guides my pen and studies me
I think he is a perfect eternity
He has me dreaming
The wild grass is weaving
I come through a portal
And he is there
I wear gossamer
Oh, darling, we are there!
We're in love now
We are roaming free
As long we can dream.

He sees me floating among the rocks
He pushes me into the silted sea floor
Breathlessly, I wait to die
But he raises me up
Like a mollusk in his mouth
Then I sink into the ooze
He drifts away quickly
My dress falls down
I float in the azure green
The sun dazzles as I wade ashore
White feathers float behind

I see a bird fly up toward the sun
Then circle and look down
I feel it watching me.

I close my eyes and dream
There is nothing for me
In my mind all the time
But our home of cedar and wine
In my heart, I long to say
Everything now has changed
In dreams we will dance
Circle high, far away.

At dawn under the trees
I am in ecstasy
Bracelets on my wrists
Music at my feet
I am sleepless and free
Sea birds call
You're dirty
You're late
Come here
Please hurry
Danger, danger
Me, me
Wait, wait
Then one speaks from on high and asks
What flower is this?

I am with him now
The boat rocks
We toss and turn
Hold me close
The stars are white
The palms sway

The sands shift
Love, come and stay!
I like to ride the high sea
I like waves that toss me around
I like to sway in the breeze
I like to twirl and fall down
I like sorrowful sounds.

He is there in the sand—
Tell me who I am!
Get on this ship of dreams, he says
And we will sail across the sea
To dance on far off shores
And then the seas were rough
And then the voyage was not a dream
But a clattering of extremes.

A soft tear fell
Just one slipped down
I was surprised—
Love is sorrow.

Early one morning
A musician knocked on my door
We walked down the cliff
I was feeling so alive!
He said, *Misery enjoys your company*
And he flashed a smile
We came up from the beach
He was breathless—
I was yearning—
He fell down on my bed
His eyes were extraterrestrial!
They spun me around!
Later that evening

He called me up to play
But he declined to remain
For months I was lost
As my heart paid the cost.

And so I began
To dance and to spin
I loved each girl
Again and again
I loved their honey eyes
I loved their thighs
I loved the sparkle in their eyes
I loved their soft long hair
I listened to their sighs
Love was in our hearts
There was wine from cups
Brought here from the south
We made love in the sand
Circled as we danced!
And when we returned
Our hearts were glowing
And when they were taken from me
My heart wasn't willing.

They cannot erase
The memory of his face
His letters are in my drawer
He entrusted his songs to me.

I wait quietly
The play begins
There are so many before us now
I am dressed in white
I pluck the strings
And begin to sing:

I want to go where
You will find me
Where we can be alone
I want no tear
No sad goodbye
I am not afraid
For the gods made love
They want us to be happy.

The pale moon shines down
I have a balanced heart
And a child inside
She is soft and resolute
The fires are burning
The thunder is clapping
I wander away
To invoke lightning
Come to me now
Set me on fire!

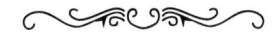

II

Now I know why Eros,
Of all the progeny of
Earth and Heaven, has
Been most dearly loved

Sappho

When I look he is there
Holding a white rose in his hand
A vagabond lover back again
And I am in the garden
With my doves in the breeze
And I say, *Oh, please*
Keep your love coming constantly
We will float this wave out to the sea.

I did not stand apart
When love came dancing down
I did not know
There could be such joy
Like geese floating on the sea.

When he plays his game
And wanders through my house again
He reminds me of a nameless cat
I feel so strong in his arms.

I say I must die
For without him
There is no song
No reason to go on
He stops me in the sand
Looks in my eyes
And kisses me—
My love will not depart
I wish to live with you
And be happy in this world.

We dream into the night
We travel through time
I play every role for him
Please lie down
And love me again
Come bring your flowing spirt
Into the light of dawn
Come, I see you clearly
Your heat burns through me
You strip away my doubt
In the early light of dawn
In the clouds that float by
Love, you are so near!

Do not waste your time
On things that trouble your mind
On those who are unkind
Free yourself from those ties
Let us take to the sky
Find solace in the breeze
In the cool dark night
Please come to me
I will make you happy.

This girl last night
Was burning bright
Now she is sad
When you are sad
She is as well
When you are sad
She suffers as well
When you are sad
She holds your hand.

He appears in the night
He drops at my feet
He watches me closely
He tickles my ears
He pushes me down
Love, you will never lose me
I am here tonight
In a world of dreams
In the day I will draw near
And I will lie in the sand
I will sway as you pass
I will touch up against you
I will circle around
I will take your hand
I will look into your eyes
Love, I am here
I will bring you a glass
However did you find me?

And as I go to sleep
I hear him say
Come and love me now
Though I am far away
Tomorrow, my love
I am on my way

Deep in heaven I am
Take my hand
Two blackbirds make loud cries
And this is me with you
And it is dawn again
I will fly to you tonight
You will find me again.

Please do not wish to die
We will never say goodbye
I know the reason why
I will stay with you
Or turn to dust
Oh, my love
I am on this road
I do not slow
Everything is shifting
Like the ground under me
Come slip away with me
The music is fine
As is the wine
We will hold each other
Through the night.

I have returned to the sea
It rings in my ears
There is something to say
On this windswept day
Two birds are fighting on the beach
Desperate days lie beyond our shores
There are cracks in the ceiling
There are caves below
We go out into the bright sunlight
And glow within its fire
This is no devastating fall

This is a place to land
In clouds of golden sand
So shall it be
Time means nothing to me
I close my eyes and dream
There is nothing for me
But our home of stucco and wine
In my heart, I long to say
Everything now has changed
They think you mad
To have a queen
Who reaches from so far away
Who follows you out into the day
Who sleeps with you at night
They do not know
You do not care
You can breathe the air
Welcome her in
And watch her go free
I want your love
You are so close
But just out of my reach
Do not look back
Come on to my path
Come to me!

His voice is soft and clear
Please take me far away from here
Love is a nightmare
That never leaves
I have no rest
I walk on fire
I hang on a wire
Do what you will
I love you

And as I go to bed
I hear him say
Come and love me again
Though I am far away
Tomorrow, love
I am on my way
Deep in heaven I am
Come take apart my heart
And tell me those things you did
Come take apart my love
I will turn and say nothing.

When love rushes in
She rushes in like the surf
She is a thing of beauty
She is a channel to the universe
Oh, just to be with you
Is my fervent desire
Every year is harder
Every year is slower
Under the sun.

Three months, three moons, is not so long
I'll bring in flowers and avoid the sun
I'll take a walk and wait for you
In the next full moon, I'll see you too
In dreams, we'll fly up to the peak
Wrapped in feathers, we'll be so unique
Stars above and the valley below
We'll meet our dreams in the dry empty void
I will let you know when I'm alone
I'll put up a garland for the holy days
I'll set up a table with trays of paint
I'll gold leaf your beautiful iconic face
And then I'll pray for snow or rain

The jackals will cackle every day
I'll visit the owl in her deadly lair
I'll hide away, I will beware
I'll pray for my muse and wait with care
I'll meditate nightly until she appears
I'll obey my soul and answer your prayer.

I'll love you forever and never forget
How beautiful you were in the sunset
Your precious kind spirit, your thoughtfulness
The times you caught me when I was upset
The dry rivers you and I stumbled upon
The voice in the wilderness calling us home
Please lie with me whenever you please
My heart is wide open, I stagger and repeat
Please rest on my arm as the night birds call
The dove hides away and the owl breaks the dawn
I'll guide you gently and put you to bed
And then I'll repeat every word that you said
You seek out the zygote, you seek out the lamb
I hold you gently, for you are my man
I have a clear mind and a pen that scrawls
I love each thigh, the way that you sprawl
You are my love, and I take the fall
Your sundial heart shines so majestically
I'll take you to heaven if you will let me
I love the sun dragon, I chase it relentlessly
I love you as well, for you are my everything.

I did not let go
I watched the dawn
I watched the fall
I saw to the heart of it all
I stepped into omega
I saw the years of fate

You lifted the veil and let me in
My feet are broken on the ground
You are my reason for being
You are my final dream
The gods are watching
The demons are listening
I see our future
And it is glistening.

Maybe there is something you want to say
About our endless share of sorrow
And all I want to say is
Your love never leaves me alone
Be careful where you go now
And barricade your door
Lose that demon, darling
And you'll lose the war
Come now, darling
I'll put you to bed
I'll read a story
Running through your head
I'll write a song
About our love in the great beyond
It's love every day, darling
With you by my side
And it's love that blinds me
When I spin and dive
Sleeping with the demon
Lock the door
Remember what happened
Just the night before
Is there something, darling
You want to say?
Erase her name, darling
We're starting a new page

A lot of people want you
To let our love go
But I think you know
It is time to write our lines
Before we fall apart
Lay your cheek upon my thigh
Love is not a crime
I'm not saying goodbye
Once I was falling
And you caught me with your song
Oh, my love
Your cheeks are so kissable
Your eyes are unmissable!

I did not tell you—
We were walking down the street
And moved aside
To let them go by
Then they spat words at me
I did not understand
We stopped holding hands
They whispered in my ear
He is so young and beautiful!
You should be ashamed!
I do not know what else they said
And I do not care
I am ready to die in your arms.

Oh, my darling
The hill is high
The stakes are higher still
Will they arrest me at your border?
Will they incinerate me later?
Oh, just to be with you
Is my fervent desire

Every year is harder
Every year is slower.

There is a house in my dreams
Where love lives in tranquility
You are so far from me
But my love remains the same.

III

With his venom
Irresistible and bittersweet
That loosener of limbs, Love
reptile-like
strikes me down

Sappho

It was a dream—
The sand, the wind, the future
My eyes are prisms now
I am in the universe
Where love began
I hold on for one more ride
I am your kind
Am I irrelevant now?
Am I going blind?
Am I seeing double?
I watch the centers come and go
You say I'll be alright
You say, whispering
What are you thinking?
I'm not leaving
Everything is fine
Please keep relaxing
No need to be asking

I wake with a racing heart
His love is out of reach!
Should I fall into the sea?
I say, *Leave if you will*
The most convenient way
I don't need it anyway
There is nothing left to say.

I'm through with love
All at once the flame dies
And the dust flies
The moon fades
The tide pulls away
The sun sets on desire
Though we may not touch
I am with him
Though we may never meet again
My love is with him
We had a dream
It was defiled
It fell upon the ground.

Going through old papers
In an antique desk
In my summer house
My brother says
Don't touch the papers!
Let them stay in the dark!
But they are not his
I want to leave
I want to dissolve
I tell him
Leave me alone!
It is my desk, after all!
I tread softly in the day

Stay silent, far away
My affliction has no cure
Who is there with him
When he dances and feeds on wine
And when he falls apart?
I am in misery
Do not come near me
The pain lingers
Unkind words were said.

I cannot sleep
I need a cure—
I'll find a place
To ease my pain
And there I'll remain
I'll wait for a sign
Then open the door
And he will be there
I have a heart
So please walk in
I have a song
Let me kiss you
Let's make amends
With one simple line
I cannot make love stay
But I can lay myself down.

If I cry in the rain
It has nothing to do with you
You are not to blame
You bring me sprigs of cedar
And you try to ease my pain
But I am not happy
And the wind blows just the same
I am so alone

I don't know why
But I loved the way
He threw flowers around
And left his books
Lying on the ground.

I do not understand love's game
She is better off not here
Where my blood is real
I bring her incense
And try not to cry—
It is the season of disguise
I am so unhappy
And there is nothing to be done
The wind keeps howling
And I want to die
Rain is pouring in the valley
I say I'm sorry—
I have to leave
I can't take it anymore!

There are angels out there
And you will be alright
You left me here
But never mind
I did not fit into your time
You cast stones to see
Who was at fault
And they chose me
You did not think me worth your while
I sometimes thought you could see me
You had an occasional look in your eye
But you could never really smile.

My clothes are strewn all over
Like my useless medicine
I know every line
To say my heart is broken
There was a time
I never wanted to leave
But now I flap my wings
I'm through with love
All at once the flame dies
And my heart is torn and broken.

It's a big world to travel
And you'll get by somehow
I'll have been your lover
You'll remember me once in awhile
I'll spend my days wounded
On the ground.

In the morning
In the ink-blue sky
I see the stars
And want to cry
I see a graveyard of smiles.

How do I mute a poet?
One in particular
Is a stab to my heart
The one I loved
But I am quiet now
I am replaced
It is easily arranged.

IV

Day in
Day out
I hunger and
I struggle

Sappho

There is a bad moon
Rising in this land
They're coming after us
They're coming soon
The people bow down
The war is in town
Their debates never cease
The poets leave the stage
And the madmen appear
I hear them whisper
I hear their drums
I hear the screams—
I must leave.

I exit when told
I do not protest
I cover up quickly
I leave with the rest
Why are they so angry?
I pray for deliverance

We are treated cruelly
No one stands for us
We feel their scorn
As we embark to leave
They rob us blind.

The world is burning
Who is to blame?
They have knives drawn
Ashes are all we are fed
I sleep with vultures
I'm a flame in the fire
An ash in a funeral pyre.

They are fighting this war
With no thought of tomorrow
They are always ready for more
In our camp
The furnishings blow in the wind
I hear birds in the morning chirping
They sing:
Please don't worry
Go back to sleep
When you wake
Life will be easy.

Were you there when they came?
Did you see the city fall?
The man had a blade
And he cut their throats
He burned their tents
He made them choke
When they woke with the dead
Did their hearts pound?

When the innocent bathe in blood
Is the war over now?

Breathe in and breathe out
Oh, my darling
Soon you will be here!
We will float out to sea
We will talk of everything
And then we'll reach Sicily!

V

*Prosperity that
the golden Muses
gave me was no
delusion: dead, I
won't be forgotten*

Sappho

The silence is welcoming
Silence is always speaking
The hummingbirds return
Death is coming quickly
Words flow, memories swarm
Waves spill their myths
Every day I am sad
Then I remember to forget
Then a song shatters everything
Love remains my dearest friend.

I've lost count of how many cups I need
You come and place one in my hand
And sometimes I am out of reach
I will sleep and then expire.

The wind is howling
It has driven me mad
The demons are screaming

The darkness is descending
The doors open to dread
The sun is blocked out
And the stone is finally rolled in
Cracks appear where I lie
My head is wrapped tightly
And there is something inside me—
An anointment, or is it a curse?

Now I am on the river
On my way into the dark
One chaste owl is hooting
We will row away
To a better place
It won't be long
My mind is on you
My eyes are as well
In a thousand years
You will find me
Over the cliff
Is where I will be
I live in the sea
Where lovers leap.

Made in United States
North Haven, CT
14 February 2024